Dr *[signature]*

A NEW KIND of NORMAL

DR. GREG PURSLEY

A NEW KIND of NORMAL

A Family's Understanding *of* Dwarfism

TATE PUBLISHING
AND ENTERPRISES, LLC

A New Kind of Normal
Copyright © 2014 by Dr. Greg Pursley. All rights reserved.

No part of this publication may be reproduced, stored in a retrieval system or transmitted in any way by any means, electronic, mechanical, photocopy, recording or otherwise without the prior permission of the author except as provided by USA copyright law.

The opinions expressed by the author are not necessarily those of Tate Publishing, LLC.

Published by Tate Publishing & Enterprises, LLC
127 E. Trade Center Terrace | Mustang, Oklahoma 73064 USA
1.888.361.9473 | www.tatepublishing.com

Tate Publishing is committed to excellence in the publishing industry. The company reflects the philosophy established by the founders, based on Psalm 68:11,
"The Lord gave the word and great was the company of those who published it."

Book design copyright © 2014 by Tate Publishing, LLC. All rights reserved.
Cover design by Rtor Maghuyop
Interior design by Gram Telen

Published in the United States of America

ISBN: 978-1-63063-142-0
1. Biography & Autobiography / General
2. Family & Relationships / Family Relationships
14.02.24

Dedication

To my wonderful wife and fantastic children. Without them I would not be the person I am today.

Acknowledgments

Thank you to all of the medics, doctors, nurses, surgeons, physical therapists, family, friends, groups, organizations, and all of the other people that have helped with keeping Izaac with us. There are so many people to thank and we appreciate every single one of you.

Contents

Foreword.. 11
What Is Normal Really? 13
May 8, 2012 17
   The day Izaac was born 17
New Normal 21
Little Days and Big Days................................... 27
Worry 31
   Sometimes Hindsight Is 20/10 35
Chivalry Is Not Dead 39
     Give Kids the World................................. 42
     Random Acts of Kindness 43
A Simple Car Ride 47
Izaac 51
    Zero to One... 51
    One to Two.. 61
    Two to Three... 64
    Three to Four 66
Normal People Problems 69
What Is Dwarfism? 73

Our Successful Relationship 77
What We Have Learned... 83
Life's Purpose 87

Foreword

This remarkable book by Dr. Gregory Pursley takes us on a journey helping us to understand dwarfism plus the untold complications that daily threatened the young life of their newborn son, Izaac. It also offers a fascinating picture of two loving parents committed to overcoming the daily challenges in caring for their baby boy. As their captivating story unfolds you are an eye witness to this heroic couple's self-sacrificing perseverance. They are forced to face down their fears all too often while caring for Izaac during his many near fatal traumatic episodes.

It's hard for anyone to imagine going through a similar experience. However, Dr. Pursley's attitude never waivers. According to Greg, if you don't experience adversity in life you won't grow and your life will be imperfect. His advice is to push through and be strong. It is a lesson we all need to learn in preparation for the many unknowns lying ahead in our own lives.

As you experience dwarfism along with Izaac's other unique problems you will have a front row seat witnessing Greg and Sheree's courage as they face their unknowns.

The power behind their personal experience is their unfailing determination to remain strong. All through this extraordinary story you can't help but notice the exceptional love they share. There is little doubt that their love gave them the strength to meet these challenges head on. Together, they continue to live the American Dream in their "new normal" world.

—Senator Wayne Wallingford

Are you selfless enough to love someone more than yourself? Even if it means becoming someone you never thought you could be? Having a child with special needs will jolt you into that role. It can be a daunting task, but also a lifelong rewarding experience. Those whom GOD chooses to take on this task are truly angels among us. In a moment you will meet and learn about a family I have known for several years, who epitomize sacrifice and total commitment. They survive the unthinkable and come out stronger every time. As you turn the pages of this book really try to imagine yourself in these predicaments and stop to absorb the enormity of life and death situations if they happened even once in your child's life. May you learn to respect people who are different as created by GOD. And may you resume your life without judgment off all people with special needs.

—Faune Riggin, Radio Personality

What Is Normal Really?

Normal is defined as conforming to the standard or the common type; usual; not abnormal; regular; natural or serving to establish a standard. The funny thing about this phenomenon of "normal" is that we are all unique, different, or special in some way. We have heard these thousands of times: "Don't judge a book by its cover," "It is what is on the inside that counts," and "Everyone is special in their own unique way." Is there anyone who actually lives by these sayings? Even in my situation, spending countless days in the hospital, visiting with hundreds of different people with a range of illnesses, it is hard to see someone for who they really are.

My wife Sheree and I were married in 2004, and like most people we envisioned a future of love, success, and children. Our relationship had always moved quickly. We met in February of 2004, engaged in July of 2004, and married in September of 2004. It seems like we just had known each other forever. We clicked on every level, and I can honestly say that through everything that we have gone through we love each other more than ever. After our first year of marriage, we had bought a car, a house, and Sheree was seven months pregnant.

We were very happy. We didn't have a huge house or all of the money in the world, but we were making it together—just the two of us. I would say, "You and me, kid" and Sheree would reply, "Me and you." In December 2005 our daughter, Evee-Kay, was born. We were and still are the proudest parents. Our little redheaded angel was the sweetest thing we had ever seen. Once again, Sheree and I were so happy. At the time that Evee-Kay was born, I was still in chiropractic school and it was finals week. Talk about a tough week. Sheree had gone through eighteen hours of labor and then had to have an emergency C-section. I felt so bad for her. I thought at the time that this would have to be the hardest thing we would ever have to face. Boy was I wrong.

At the time, we were getting by. Sheree was working and supporting the family and I had to learn to control my pride. I graduated in the spring of 2006 from chiropractic college. I didn't really know what I was going to do at the time or where I was going to end up. I just think that life sometimes points you in the right direction for whatever reason. I am a firm believer in the idea that everything happens for a reason…if you can accept everything that happens.

A New Kind of Normal

In November of 2006, I opened my practice. It was a huge risk for us. We moved two hours away from our family and started a business. Sheree quit her job in St. Louis and didn't have a job in this new location. To make matters worse, if the business failed, so did we. After three months, I realized I had no idea on how to run a business, so I went to California for two weeks to study about the importance of implementing systems. Once again, I thought that this would be the hardest time of my life, but I found out that I was very wrong. I came back having been away from my family for two weeks with new perspective and ideas. The only down side was I now had to implement everything that I had learned. This took even more time from Sheree and Evee-Kay. The good news is after a lot of hard work the business grew, so once again everything was going our way. In the fall of 2007, Sheree got pregnant again and we were ecstatic. We actually found out after we got home from Disney world. Here we were a family of three with a successful business in a nice home, going to have another baby to make us a family of four. We were literally going to be living the American dream.

The pregnancy went great and there were no hiccups to it. Sheree and I took the right precautions. She ate right and took vitamins; we worked out and stayed in shape. Looking back, I don't think that we did a single thing wrong during the pregnancy. At twenty weeks, we got an ultrasound and found out the baby was a boy. We would now have one girl and one boy. Once again, the American dream lives on. I could see our future, all four of us living life having so much fun along the way, just being the "perfect" family. This is what most people envision for their family's life, and we were no different. Everything was falling into place just like we had planned, but then remember plans don't always go like you think they will.

May 8, 2012

The day Izaac was born

The day Izaac was born was an exciting one. Sheree and I had our family's down for the delivery and we had a friend come up from Houston. Our whole family was excited with anticipation. Since Sheree had a C-section with Evee-Kay, she had to have a scheduled C-section with Izaac. We all got up at five in the morning, packed all of our things in the car and drove up to the hospital without any drama, screaming or anything that the movies actually portray. We got to the hospital and checked in. The nurse escorted us to our room, which was very spacious and nicer than we had thought it would be. They came in and prepped Sheree for surgery. At seven o'clock, a nurse wheeled her to the operating room and sent me to prepare to sit in. I had to stay outside the surgery door until they got her ready. I was sitting in full scrubs from head to toe. I just remember being so excited and nervous about our second child. I do remember feeling different about this delivery. I think maybe it was because I knew what to expect after watching Sheree go through a C-section with our first child, but still something felt different.

At 7:05, they brought me back to the room where Sheree was prepped and ready to go. After a couple of tests, they were off. I remember the doctor talking about American Idol with Sheree which seemed to calm her nerves. It was really that calm and relaxed, no big deal. Then after about fifteen minutes, the doctor said, "Okay, are you guys ready?" With a little suction cup and a couple of tugs, Izaac Gregory Pursley was born. I saw him immediately after he came out and I remember feeling like he looked a little different, but as a parent wanting everything to be perfect I thought what a beautiful baby boy. I couldn't have been more excited.

Immediately the nurses took Izaac to get cleaned up as they finished up with Sheree. There was a glass panel where I could see what was going on. Once again I thought to myself "Something seems different" and once again I discounted it saying "Well, this is a different hospital than where Evee-Kay was born." After a little while Izaac was brought back to our room. We were filled with the kind of joy that only new parents can feel. We were visiting with family, laughing, chatting, and catching up when a doctor came in and asked to speak with Sheree and I. She said "Would it be ok with everyone if I spoke with Mom and Dad?" Naturally everyone agreed and slowly exited the room. After everyone had exited the room the doctor pulled up a chair, sat down, and took a deep breath. I want to talk to you about baby Izaac. There are a couple of things I want to point out."

Immediately panic came over Sheree and I. "Things? What things?" I said very nervously. It was a feeling of nervousness, anxiety, panic, and fear all rolled in to one. The doctor began to explain her findings. She said "It is very likely that Izaac has a form of dwarfism." She pointed out how his forehead protruded out slightly (frontal bossing), how his upper arms and legs were shorter than average, and how his first three fingers were the same length (trident fingers). Later on we found out he had Achondroplasia.

At this point Sheree and I were in pure shock. None of this was expected or planned for, but then again, what in life is?

See picture 1 on page 93

I think in life, it is human nature to think nothing bad will happen to you. Look at all of the people on television who have something horrific happen to them they always say, "I didn't think it would happen to me." I think we all have a thought about what our life will be like in one year, in five years, in ten years, and so on. Just sit back and think about it. It is amazing how you won't think about anything bad in life. It will only be the good times and good things that you will think of. The fact is if we don't have adversity in life we won't grow, and life is imperfect. So my advice to anyone who is facing adversity is to push through and be strong. Try to find the lesson in what you are facing. The more things you get through in life, the stronger and more prepared you become for what lies ahead.

I heard a story one time about tadpoles and I think it sums up what I am trying to say. The natural lifecycle of a tadpole is to grow legs and turn into a frog. However, if you take a tadpole and put it in a bowl of water with smooth edges, it will never grow legs. The fact is it will just keep swimming around in this bowl forever never growing legs. Why? There is no need to grow legs if there is nothing to climb on. Now if you take a rock and put it in the middle of the bowl where the top of the rock is poking above the water, then the tadpole will bump into the rock and will start to develop legs. Why does this happen? Well, it is just like life. If the tadpole doesn't have an obstacle to overcome, it will never fully develop and mature. In a human's life, if everything is just handed to them and they never have to earn anything, they will never mature or develop. So when things come your way, just think to yourself this is going to make you stronger and it will make you a better person. Personally, I have been through a lot, but looking back it has given me clarity and compassion toward other people's situations due to the fact that I can relate. If I didn't take the time to step back and look at what I have learned from the trials in my life, I would feel bitter and angry about what has "happened" to me.

New Normal

Looking back to the day that Izaac was born is hard. There were such mixed emotions. Not that I was upset he was different, but I was scared he would not be able to experience life. Parts of me were selfish. Why did I have a child with something *wrong* with him? Looking back on it now, I have to laugh. That child—the child who had something wrong with him—taught me what was wrong with me. I remember the day Izaac was born Sheree holding him. I wrapped my arms around them and she started to tear up. "What about you playing sports with your son," she said as she started to cry. As a man I knew, I could not break down. I looked at her and said, "Today is a happy day," and that was the end of that. I had my struggles with staying strong; I had my doubts about holding it all together. There were times I had to retreat the bathroom or hallway to hide my emotion.

The fact is when we are thrown into situations, we can either succumb to them or rise above them, and succumbing to this was not an option.

As the days went by, Izaac was like any other baby. The future started to look bright. Yeah, he was going to be different, but then again who isn't? We went to a couple of checkups and everything looked great. We were informed that there were complications to look out for with a dwarf child. We took it in stride always hoping for the best. Some of the complications included hydrocephalus (swelling of the brain), spinal stenosis (narrowing of the spinal column), uncoordinated suck/swallow response, lung compression, and joint problems.

When Izaac was three months old, we went in for a routine sleep study to make sure that he was holding oxygen. This didn't seem like such a big deal. A one night sleep study to help ease our minds, or so we thought. A couple of days later the results were in and we found out Izaac would need oxygen at night because he would stop breathing from time to time. So we went and picked up oxygen tanks and got all the necessary equipment. We also needed to have Izaac on a pulse oximeter, which measures oxygen; an apnea belt, which measures breathing; and an apnea mat, which measures motion. All three of these machines had their own separate alarm. You can assume that we did not get much sleep after that. We were waking up every fifteen to thirty minutes to respond to an alarm. The boy-who-cried-wolf principle could not be applied here either. Every alarm startled you because it only takes one real alarm happening to make you never miss another alarm.

A New Kind of Normal

See picture 2 on page 93

See picture 3 on page 94

In between getting his sleep study at three months old and having a long-term stay, Izaac had three multiple day stays in the hospital. Each time he was given breathing treatments and we were told it was a cold. Come to find out later on, Izaac was aspirating food. This means he literally was breathing in his milk and we didn't even know it. Now it is hard to watch home videos of this time in our life because we can see he was in pain. He would drink his bottle which is normally something a parent can stare at in awe without worry. Little did we know he was literally injuring his lungs with every drink. To this day, I regret not knowing this was happening.

Izaac had two stints in the hospital, one for six weeks and one for three months. The six week stint started in the fall of the fall of 2008 when Izaac was just six months old and Sheree and Evee-Kay went up to St. Louis. Sheree's grandfather had passed away and they were going to go to the funeral. I had to stay behind and wait until the work week ended. The first night Sheree was in St. Louis, Izaac started having breathing difficulties. He was crying and in a lot of pain. I can only imagine what Sheree was going through. She kept upping his oxygen, more and more until it was at full blast. Four liters is like breathing pure oxygen and Izaac still couldn't keep his levels of oxygen up in his blood. She called me in a panic. Hysterically, she said "Izaac won't stop crying and I don't know what to do. I think I am going to have to take him to the hospital." I was still talking with her as she and her mom loaded him into the car. She was crying the whole time. The next thing I heard from her was that Izaac had to be intubated (a tube to help him breathe). She said he had stopped breathing and a doctor had to do chest compressions until they got the breathing tube in. Sheree was told he lost oxygen for a while, and we will have to wait and see in the morning if his brain was functioning or not. Sheree called me after all of this and said, "Your son is dying. You need to come up here." Immediately, my adrenaline spiked and I hopped in the car to go to St. Louis. That was the longest two-hour drive of my life. In those two hours I foolishly played out every possible scenario in my head. With no one to talk to, I sat in silence as I thought of the possibilities. My emotions were uncontrollable.

When I finally arrived at the hospital, they had Izaac strapped to the table and he was sleeping due to the medications. Massive pneumonia they said. If you had waited any longer to get him here, he wouldn't have made it. We always thank Papa for saving Izaac's life. If we would not have been there for his funeral, we would not have gotten Izaac to a hospital in time. That night, my parents stayed by Izaac's side while we went to Papa's wake.

Unbeknownst to my wife or any of the family, I leaned over and silently I thanked him for saving my son's life.

Have you ever been forced to be somewhere that you didn't want to be? Imagine being a family-oriented man forced to be two hours away from your son and wife who are in a hospital and your daughter who is somewhere with a family member. Think about someone you love being in the hospital while you have to go to work. Owning my own business at that time in my life was a curse. I resented having to go to work. I resented having to be somewhere where I couldn't help my family. Money was becoming tighter every day. I went home to an empty house every night during the week and went to the hospital on the weekends. I would stay at the hospital all weekend, so Sheree could go to her mom's to get some sleep. I really don't know how she was able to stay by his side every day. She is definitely stronger than she thinks she is. Somehow, against all odds, we came together as a family and made it work this is something I think more families should do in our society today.

Little Days and Big Days

The daily grind can sometimes seem too long and too repetitive. Everyone experiences this in life in one way or the other. My day starts off, not with one alarm or a slow progression of waking up, but with multiple alarms attached to my son, Izaac. There is the pulse oximeter which measures pulse rate and oxygen level in the blood and is attached to his toe. One of the favorite things that he does is to take it off and make it alarm because he knows we will come and check on him. This alarm sounds like a slightly high-pitched tone and alarms in sets of three—*Boop, boop, boop!...boop, boop, boop!* My eyes open quickly with a thought, *Is this his oxygen level dropping or him taking the cord off of his toe?* Not the best first question of the day. The other alarm is with his ventilator, also known as portable life support. A thirty-five-pound, awkward rectangle on top of a metal stand with five roller legs attached at the bottom. The stand weighs around twenty pounds and holds his vent, oxygen tank, and heater/humidifier machine. The humidifier attached to the stand has a sterile water bag feeding it water. If one of the four heat sensors come off of the tubing that is attached to the vent and my son, then it will also alarm. The heater alarm is quieter and less alarming than the other two but is still very annoying. It alarms in sets of four starting with a deeper sound to a higher pitched sound and repeats itself every 5 seconds. Boop, boop, boop, boop. The vent alarm however is a high-pitched, piercing, consistent, and rhythmic sound that can be heard from the other end of the house. This alarm goes off if Izaac coughs, laughs, talks, sneezes, becomes disconnected from the vent tubing, runs, trips, stands up, or anything else interrupting the flow of air coming from the vent to his lungs. Needless to say, this alarm goes off hundreds of times throughout the day. The sound reminds me of an industrial truck or bus backing up.

So my day starts and I walk into Izaac's room.

After making sure his alarming isn't life threatening I said, "Good morning Buddy."

His response? "Eat." He's not very subtle.

"Well Izaac, let's get you into the living room so we can cook some breakfast." This may sound like an easy task, but there is a little more difficulty taking a thirty-seven-pound child attached to over a hundred pounds of equipment a hundred feet to the other room. So the next step is convincing Izaac that we need to go to the kitchen to start cooking breakfast. Generally, he is a little crabby when waking up, like most four-year-olds, so there is some resistance.

"Izaac," I said, "if you would like to eat breakfast, then we need to go to the living room so I can watch you while I cook some sausage and pancakes (his favorite)."

"Otay," he says back as he rolls off of his bed.

Meanwhile, I frantically unplugged his nebulizer, oxygen concentrator, ventilator, and humidifier. I then grab his suction unit and put it on my shoulder, his red bag which has all of his lifesaving equipment, put it on like a backpack, roll all of the cords up that are attached to his equipment, pick Izaac up with my left arm and drag his vent stand with my right. I try to be as quiet as possible as to not wake up my wife, Sheree, and my daughter, Evee-Kay, but any little hiccup and the vent alarm goes off. Like I said, this is the loud alarm that is piercing. After making it to the living room the first task is to reattach everything to power sources and appropriate places. The vent, humidifier, oxygen tubing, red bag, and suction machine all need to be put back in their place. This process of getting him out of bed and transferring him into the living room generally takes about thirty minutes.

Everyone has a morning routine that is pretty consistent, but most can choose what they would like to do. People who have children have less choice than those who don't. People who have special needs children have no choice; they are bound by the needs of the special individuals that have come in to their lives. It is easy to look at the situation and say woe is me, but I can choose to ask myself a better question with a better answer. What is great about my situation? The answer is that Izaac is still here and as inconvenient as the alarms are, at least there is someone to set them off.

I am not complaining, and I don't want to be misunderstood. I have accepted the fact of how it is and I make the most out of it every day. Like I said, he is a special individual that has made me understand the value of appreciation. The fact that my daughter is so great and has not had any major medical issues makes me even more grateful.

In life I once found myself taking the little things for granted. Like most people I was caught in a trap chasing money and status. I have come to realize a lot of little days are more important than big days. I was once caught up trying to do too much with too little and ended up taking for granted the little things right in front of me. I find it helpful to take a look at what is happening right now and to take note of all of the truly important things surrounding me. Doing this has allowed me to enjoy life more and chase life less. I appreciate life more because I know while I can plan for my future I cannot predict it. Tomorrow will come whether I like it or not, but I will not spend my tomorrow regretting what I did not cherish today. There is a saying "Yesterday is history, tomorrow is a mystery, but today is a gift. That is why it is called the present."

Worry

Having children has an unexpected feeling that goes along with the joy, excitement, and expectations. That feeling is worry. Whether you have a child that is average or not, parents will always worry about their children. I never took this into consideration before having children, but I learned in a big way that the worry of having children definitely has different layers. I have learned some children need to be worried about more than others, but the fact remains the parents still worry about their safety, well-being, and future.

Have you ever been worried? Most people worry about big issues such as; the bills getting paid, or something to do with their job. How about worried to step out of a room, go to the bathroom, sleep at night, or cook dinner? Worry can drain a person's energy and soul to the point where they are running on fumes. Worry will lead to hopelessness or depression which many individuals deal with every day. The process of the mind will change when every situation is judged and eventually the reaction or action is dictated by worry. I have seen this happen right before my eyes. My wife Sheree worries constantly. Hmmm, should I go to the store? This is no longer a one-step process. Instead, it is a multistep, hundreds of thousands of possible outcomes, brain twisting decision that would make most dizzy. Instead of just being able to go to the store she has to ask the question, will my son be okay? In fact, any decision, from taking a trip to the bathroom or simply going in the other room, everyone in the family have to ask the same question. The difference is my wife is forced to stay home to look after her child and to keep him alive which, as parents, is our responsibility.

A once wonderful tradition of going out to eat breakfast and drink coffee with her friends has become a twisted game of when can I be home, and is he going to be okay? The worry that is involved is so immense she is even scared of her phone ringing. Life has taught her if she is not at home looking at our son and the phone rings, it must be bad news. For most, they would react to the situation after it has happened, but she is now trained to react to all situations before they happen. Imagine looking at everything you do and taking the multistep thought process before you do them. Do we have the vent, suction, emergency bag, oxygen, thickener, ambu-bag, emergency trach, and are they all quickly within reach? Worrying constantly leads to exhaustion; exhaustion leads to depression, which leads to a hopeless outlook in life. There is a saying "Don't wish your life away." Life moves fast enough as it is and you don't want to wish parts of your life away. Focusing on all of the positive things and trying to live in the moment tend to reduce worry, and then being prepared for every possible situation at all times help to calm the nerves. Nevertheless, it is still harder than average.

One day, I got home from work. It was just like most days where I park my car in the garage, walk inside and go to my room to change clothes. I was in a great mood and had a skip to my step. Evee-Kay and Sheree were in the kitchen cooking dinner and Izaac was in the living room with a nurse watching him. At the time, our rule was when the vent beeps, you look at Izaac to see if he is okay first. If so, then look at the vent and see why it is beeping. If the vent beeps more than six times in a row, there is a problem. On this particular day I changed clothes, walked into the hallway, and what I saw happening will be something that I can, and will, play back in my head for the rest of my life. The nurse was kneeling over Izaac who was lying on the floor in front of the couch and I heard him say, "A little help please." The moment I heard him say that, I saw that Izaac was passed out and blue from head to toe. Immediately, adrenaline pumped through my body and without thinking I jumped into action.

"Sheree! Call 911!" I shouted as I grabbed the nurse's collar and drug him away from Izaac. Evee-Kay was talking to her grandma on the phone. Without a second thought Sheree ripped the phone out of her hand to call for help.

"Buddy! Buddy!" Okay, the vent is beeping, but why? Is the oxygen on? Is the circuit (the tubing attaching Izaac to the vent) attached? Is he breathing? Is he plugged off (When the trach is blocked by mucous)? Is his heart pumping?

I grabbed the ambu-bag (a device used to push breathes manually into the lungs) as Sheree attached it to oxygen. I picked him up in my arms and pumped the ambu-bag by hand.

I yelled, "Izaac! Izaac!" His eyes are rolled back in his head. I'm screaming frantically. "Buddy, come on!" His mouth is foaming with saliva from lack of oxygen.

"Dammit…Izaac…breathe!" After what seemed like an hour but I am sure only a couple of minutes his color started to turn from blue to pink.

A sigh of relief comes over us.

"That's right Buddy, stay with me," as his eyes started to blink slowly and his pupils constricted.

A tear rolled down my cheek as he whimpered almost as if he was in pain…and then he smiled slightly. Just then the ambulance showed up with two paramedics. They rushed in with all of their equipment and started asking us what the problem was. "I don't know, I think it was the ventilator malfunctioning." They checked his vitals and everything looked good. They asked if we would like to take him to the hospital and we said no due to the fact that he was reactive. Afterward I asked the nurse "what happened?" He mumbled around for a while until I had enough. "It was your fault wasn't it?"

"No, I don't know what happened. He just stopped breathing."

"Then you should have called for help sooner if he stopped breathing…Please leave!" I couldn't stand to see him anymore as I had a suspicion it was his fault. Come to find out later, it was his fault, even though he would not admit it.

People make mistakes. In fact mistakes are what we learn from. It is okay to tell someone that you made a mistake and apologize for it. Just make sure you learn something from the mistake that was made.

This may sound ridiculous and scary, but this is just one of many close calls we have had. Even with everything he has gone through, he is still one of the happiest people I have ever met.

Sometimes Hindsight Is 20/10

As young parents experiencing everything for the first time all over again, we made our decisions based on what we thought was right at the time, or what we thought was not risky. Our reality of life at the time was very skewed though. One time Sheree and I decided we wanted to go to an employee appreciation bonfire at a golf course we used to work at. As most parents do we went to the grandparents and said "Can you watch our kids tonight so we can go to the party?"

"Of course," replied my parents. "We would love to."

So we dropped the kids off and headed out to the party which was about thirty-five minutes away. At this time, Izaac was only five months old and had been on oxygen for the last two months through a nasal cannula. We had enough oxygen to last for days, a pulse ox, and an emergency bag. We felt confident and my parents were fine with us going to the event. Before we left, we made a statement that at the time seemed harmless enough.

"If he starts to turn blue, just roll him over to his side, turn his oxygen up, pat his back, and he'll be fine." Today this statement sounds absurd and totally ridiculous, but at the time it was our "normal," our reality—all that we knew.

As prepared as we all thought we were, you can never be prepared for everything. At some point in the night, Izaac started to have some distress with breathing. Abiding by the rules that we had set, his Grandpa and Grandma rolled him to his side, turned the oxygen up, and patted him on the back. The problem was in the oxygen tank. It malfunctioned and was not delivering oxygen through the nasal cannula. Izaac's oxygen continued to drop and he was turning blue. I cannot begin to explain to them how sorry I am for the selfish decision of leaving him there. My parents decided to do the only thing that they knew how to do—Call 911. Luckily, they live in a small town and help arrived quickly to save Izaac's life. They brought in extra oxygen, put a mask on him, and gave him manual breaths until he came to. The reaction from his body was the same as every other time that he had lost oxygen. When he loses oxygen, he foams at the mouth, his eyes roll in the back of his head, and he goes limp. When he is revived, he is extremely tired, lethargic, and crabby. I can't really understand what he is feeling because I have never passed out before, but from my experiences with him it does not look very pleasant. When we got home my parents cautiously asked, "Does Izaac lose oxygen a lot?"

This sparked the question from us, "Why, what happened?"

They went on to tell us what exactly happened. To my parents, this incident hit especially close to home. When I was two years old, they lost a son due to a farming accident at three years old. I am sure they had flashbacks after what they experienced with Izaac that night.

At the time if there was an issue with Izaac's oxygen tank, whether it ran out or there was a malfunction, you had about thirty seconds to rectify the situation. After thirty seconds his oxygen would drop from the mid 90's percentage wise into the 60's. Like I said, we did what we thought was best at the time.

Our lives are made up by decisions. One decision leads to another…and another…and another. You are who you are today because of the decisions you have made in the past and the decisions you make every moment. We decided to take a measured risk that, at the time, didn't seem dangerous.

Looking back we see how dangerous it was. We could have played the blame game and said it was someone else's fault that he had a problem, but that never gets anyone anywhere. My advice to anyone is learn from your decisions so you can correct in the future and become a better person. We owned up to the fact that we made a bad decision, and in learning from that decision we were able to make changes to how we do things which has saved Izaac's life many times. If we had missed out on the opportunity, we would never have made changes, and our relationship with my parents would have been strained. The moral of the story is use what happens and remember that the only way to change your future is to change the decisions that you make today.

Chivalry Is Not Dead

I have heard the statement "Chivalry is dead." In this country, we have the problem of focusing on the negative side of situations. With all of the news and media focusing their attention on primarily negative things, it is hard to see there are still amazing people out there doing amazing things. These are individuals who are always standing on guard to keep the balance of good and bad in the world. If we were to look around us and forget what this world has trained us to do, we would be able to see the unbelievable good deeds happening around us every day. Unfortunately, this is not the case for most. Most people watch the news, listen to the radio, read stories online, and listen to gossip which all just fuels the unquenchable fire of negativity. We have encountered these people and through our son, we have been given the gift of viewing the world with a new perspective—one of kindness, hope, and positivity. Izaac is such an inspiration simply because he smiles in every situation. Sure he is still a child who comes with the occasional whine or fit, but his overall outlook in life is positive. This child has been through more than most people could imagine, and he walks around with a smile on his face. If you open your eyes and look around, it is not hard to see the good that surrounds you.

I remember the joy on my wife's face the day that she found out we could apply for a Make-A-Wish trip. The expression of joy was one that we rarely had due to our situation. We told a few people and were met with the question.

 I thought Make-a-Wish was for terminal children.

Our reply was, "Well, he is on a ventilator to help him breathe."

I remember thinking, *Has our society lost the ability to be genuinely happy for another person without being cynical?*

Izaac was approved for his trip based on the fact that we didn't know whether or not his lungs would grow or not. If his lungs don't grow and his body does, he either becomes dependent on the vent full time or he won't be able to provide his body with oxygen. We know where that leads.

Make-A-Wish was fantastic through every step of the process. It is primarily a volunteer organization. On two occasions, volunteers drove to our house from over an hour away to help us through the process of filling out paperwork and answering questions. On the day the wish was approved, they came to our house with balloons and really made a big deal out of it. They interviewed Izaac, who was two at the time, and only got one word, "Mickey."

My wife started to tear up. When Izaac was six months old, he had a six-week stay in the hospital and a three-month stay when he was nine months old. The days that he was intubated (a ventilator going in to his lungs through his mouth), tied down to the bed, and sedated with meds, Sheree would sit next to him for hours rubbing his head and saying, "When you get through this, I am taking you to Disney world." They would watch Mickey Mouse Clubhouse together at the hospital and even though Izaac was sedated, he would still manage to move his little head and kick his little feet.

The Make-A-Wish organization decided they would pay for us to fly to Florida and stay at Give Kids The World Village. Disney and Universal gave all of us free passes to their theme parks and an indoor skydiving business named IFly gave us a free package for four.

The Make-A-Wish organization was there every step of the way from the moment we showed up at the airport until the moment we got back. They had people greet us everywhere we went and had everything figured out. Their goal is to give the family a moment to remember without worry or fear. I look forward to helping this group in the future because of the kindness and generosity they have shown, and I hope you will too.

See picture 4 on page 94

See picture 5 on page 95

Give Kids the World

In the previous section, I mentioned Give Kids the World. This is a place I had never heard of until Make-A-Wish, but it is a place that everyone should know about. Give Kids the World is a nonprofit organization run almost completely on donated food, money, and time. It is a place of giving, selflessness, and hope for families who have little to give and even less hope. It is a village—a colorful, well kept, amazing village—of games, cottages, playgrounds, ice cream, and the best human kind has to offer. It is a place where money cannot buy a room no matter what amount. Only a child, a family, and an unthinkable situation will get you invited. I am sure most families would say they would much rather have a healthy child and would never have seen Give Kids The World, until they see the joy and wonder it brings to every child's heart. I love Give Kids The World, not for what it does, which is amazing, but for what it represents. It represents kindness, giving, selflessness, and a sense of others before yourself. It is infectious and makes one think about what they could do to help others also. It doesn't have to be a child that has an illness. It could be your next door neighbor, a relative, a coworker. Every day we are given the choice to help others or to think about ourselves. At Give Kids the World, selfishness isn't even in their vocabulary.

While we were there, I noticed other families—families who would not have been able to take their child on a week-long trip without the help of these organizations. This is why I support them and, once again, I hope you will too. There is good out there, you just have to train yourself to see it.

See picture 6 on page 95

Random Acts of Kindness

One evening, Sheree and I decided our family needed a night out, just the four of us. We chose to go out to eat at Outback Steakhouse. This doesn't sound like a big deal, but when you add the complication of Izaac's medical equipment it becomes an issue. We were there for about an hour, laughing and having fun when suddenly Izaac coughed really hard a few times. Instantly, it was an emergency situation. Sheree ran out to the car and grabbed his oxygen while I hooked him up to the vent. I suctioned him a few times and Sheree hooked the oxygen to the vent as soon as she could. After, what seemed like five minutes, he was okay and sat back up. The forty or so other people on that side of the restaurant on the other hand weren't so okay. It is in a moment like this when we realize how different our lives really are. When we are living in it every day, we try to act as normal as possible, but then we are brought back to reality in a moment's notice. After the adrenaline rush, we decided to share a dessert to celebrate that we weren't headed off to the hospital. When we asked for our check the waitress said, "A gentleman picked up the check for you."

We replied, "Really? Who?"

"He asked me not to tell you."

"Tell him thank you for us please."

He didn't have to do this random act of kindness, but I guess he saw a family trying to have a night out with a complicated situation. Well, I would like to say, whoever he is, I would like to thank him for the dinner and the random act of kindness that may have touched others like it touched us. The list goes on. While we were in the hospital a family, who had a child in the NICU in the past, brought Thanksgiving dinner to everyone there and served. They took the time and money, which was hundreds of dollars, to provide a glimmer of what might be happening at home that day.

We stayed at the Ronald McDonald House which only charged five dollars per day.

It provided a room, nice bed, and at the very least, a homely environment where people can feel secure in an insecure situation. A common practice at the house was for organizations, groups, or individuals to come and cook food for the residents of the house. Donations come from all around the area and country to help families who are going through, well, hell.

A Simple Car Ride

I never thought I would enjoy being able to hop in my car without a thought and drive away. It's such a simple thing that millions of people do every day. Decide where you want to go, get in your car, and drive away. Instead we are faced with a checklist which must be performed for even the shortest trip. We call it our five-step check list. Vent? Suction Unit? Red Bag? Oxygen? and Drink? Check. Okay, now we can go.

There was one time we forgot the suction unit. I thought Sheree picked it up and she thought I picked it up, so no one picked it up. We headed to my parents' house which is about two hours away for my sister's birthday party. We are very family oriented so we try and make as many events as possible. It has been extremely hard through the years as we are faced with either disappointing our family, each other, or ourselves. We are faced with a question with each event. Will Izaac survive? That seems like a dramatic question, but it is what we are faced with.

So, we had forgotten his suction unit and we did not realize it until we were at the event. Two hours away from the suction unit. One and a half hours away from a hospital. One could imagine our stress level. We stayed for a little while but eventually the thought that all it would take is a little cough from Izaac and we would be rushing to the hospital got to us. So we decided to head home. We left in a rush from the party, and well, my family did not understand. Most people can't understand the situation that we are in, unless they have lived through it. There is a saying "Proximity is power." I first heard it from Tony Robbins. I highly recommend his training. The saying means that the closer you are to a situation, the more you understand it. We live two hours away and I can count on one hand the amount of family members that have visited. The fact is our family really only sees us when Izaac is feeling well. Due to this fact, they really cannot understand the complexities of the situation. He is happy, lively, and very entertaining when he is feeling well. The flip side of health is sickness and when he is sick it is a 180-degree turn around. It is hard for parents to understand or put themselves in our shoes, imagining life or death in every situation. It is not something most people are prepared to deal with. We simply do not have a choice on the matter. There are people who think they have a choice though. Adoption agencies are filled with children that have a form of dwarfism. There are websites strictly for adopting children with dwarfism.

Some of these families have multiple other children that are "normal" and they choose to give up their child because he/she does not fit within the status quo. It is a sad world that we live in when someone can choose to give up their child only on the basis that the child is not "perfect."

I always thought a stressful car ride with children would be yelling at them to stop fighting or saying "I will turn this care around." There is still some of that, but there is a bigger issue that we deal with. When we are in the car and Izaac falls asleep, we are terrified that his oxygen level will drop, so we constantly check on him. Every now and then, Sheree and I will start to relax and have some light conversation and then I will glance in the rearview mirror where I could see Izaac sleeping.

The light hits him just right and his color looks just a little off. "Sheree, does he look a little blue to you?" She jerks around to check on him.

"No, it is just the light."

"Oh good," I say, as my adrenaline starts to come down.

Before Izaac was two years old, he lacked the muscle tone to sit up in his car seat properly. Also, with his form of dwarfism, the lower back does not curve in, it curves out. What this means is when he sits down, the lower part of his spine collapses out and pushes back in to the car seat. After about an hour of driving, he would start to cry and then we had to worry about him passing out. So in a car ride when his back would start to hurt, he would cry and before he had his trach he would turn blue. Sheree and I would have to make quick decisions.

"Should I pull over?" I was driving seventy miles per hour on the highway.

"Yes, pull over now."

So I jerked the wheel over and got on the side of the road. I hopped out of the car and we immediately turned from parents to emergency medical personnel. There were times that we didn't have Izaac's equipment in just the right which made it harder to get it. Once again we learned from our mistakes and corrected for the next time. Unfortunately this situation happened many times. Traveling more than 30 minutes wasn't worth the stress, anxiety, or risk. We became something that we never thought we would be - home bodies.

Izaac

Zero to One

Izaac's first year is hopefully the hardest year of his entire life. I know it was the hardest year of my family's life to date. Izaac's first three months of life were relatively uneventful compared to the months that would be ahead. He was a newborn baby. He ate, pooped, cried, and woke up at night a lot. The hardest part for us was the three machines he had at the time. He had a sleep apnea monitor that was underneath his blanket. This monitored his movement. Basically, if it didn't sense any movement from breathing, it would go off. He also had a pulse oximeter on that would beep when his oxygen level dipped below ninety. Finally he had a apnea belt which wrapped around his chest. This monitored his chest rising and falling with every breath. If it didn't sense movement it would beep. For Sheree and I, that meant we slept in fifteen-minute shifts because about every fifteen minutes, one of the machines would beep. Sleep deprived does not even begin to explain how we felt. At the end of three months, his team of doctors wanted to check his sleep apnea and see to what extent it was affecting him. I have never understood a sleep apnea test. If you haven't had the pleasure of experiencing one of these, consider yourself lucky. There are wires hooked up to your head, chest, back, and toe. It monitors breathing rate, heart rate, oxygen level, and brain activity. What I don't understand about the test is how the patient can get any restful sleep out of it. The fact was it needed to be done and it showed Izaac stopped breathing often and for long durations. The doctors on his team decided he needed to have some supplemental oxygen to help keep his levels from dropping. This was the first of his medical equipment.

I never thought about looking different or being different than everyone else around me, but going out in public was now different. It was no longer, "Oh, look at the cute baby." It was now, "Oh, poor thing, what is wrong with him?"

I am not the type of person that will be embarrassed about a situation or angry at someone for asking questions but after a while it did start to get on my nerves a little bit. I did not like the thought of other people feeling sorry for me, my family, or our situation. Sheree and I were amazed at some of the comments people would make. We walked into a fast-food restaurant with Izaac on oxygen. I had the oxygen tank in a bag on my shoulder with a cord going to Izaac who was in a car seat. The place was empty as we walked up to the counter. An employee came up from the back and saw me holding the bag and the oxygen tubing coming out of it. The counter blocked her view of Izaac, who was sleeping in his car seat on the floor. Instead of saying the traditional "Welcome to——, may I take your order?" she proceeded to say, "Aren't you a little young to be hooked up to a machine?" Stunned, I tilted my head, squinted my eyes in a confused daze. I couldn't believe someone would be so brash or intrusive. So I decided the right thing to do was to pick the car seat up, put it on the counter and say, "Well, it's not for me, it's for him." The girl took a step back, put her hands on her face which showed a look of utter remorse and said, "Oh my gosh! I am so, sorry." I was very perplexed at the fact that she could make a comment to me about being on "a machine" but because it was on a baby in a car seat, she felt bad. I still don't quite understand the logic. So I did the nice thing and said it is okay and went ahead with my order. After this incident I understood how to treat everyone without bias, and I decided to make the conscious effort to treat everyone equally no matter what.

At the time we really did not realize how sick Izaac truly was. It was pretty common for him to lose oxygen when he threw a fit. The doctors didn't seem too concerned about it, but looking back I think Sheree and I were minimizing the situation. Minimizing used to be my first response to everything. It turned out the entire time Izaac was microaspirating (breathing in microscopic pieces of food). This is what causes pneumonia, which puts years of "mileage" on your lungs.

In the first six months of Izaac's life we had dozens of doctors' visits, from trying to figure out what type of dwarfism Izaac had to dealing with his sleep apnea and fighting off sinus issues. It was a very uncertain time. Every time we had to go to the doctor's office, we had to travel to St. Louis because there weren't any doctors in our area that would be able to treat Izaac's condition.

It really felt like a time bomb ready to erupt at any time. We had very few answers and mounting questions. Then, one day, it happened. Izaac had a major aspiration where he breathed in food. At the time he was only six months old. As I mentioned earlier, Sheree had taken the kids to St. Louis for her grandfather's funeral. We live about two hours outside of St. Louis and it was the middle of the week. I own a business so I stayed home. I remember the call as if it was happening right now.

Sheree called and said, "Izaac is having trouble breathing. I have his oxygen all the way up and he is still turning blue"

Sheree had her mom and Evee-Kay with her and she said, "Everyone get in the car."

On the way to the hospital I was on the phone with them the whole time. I could hear Izaac's grandma in the background, behind his cries and gasps for air. "Come on buddy, come on." She would say over and over.

A New Kind of Normal

They got to the hospital without a moment to spare. At this point, it was a full-fledged emergency. They rushed him into the ER.

The doctor and staff immediately said they will be intubating. Intubation is a tube that passes through the mouth into the airway to support breathing. The problem is Izaac's airway is smaller than usual due to his dwarfism. I can only imagine the scene from what Sheree has told me. She had to feel as alone as anyone could feel in this moment as her son was on a table with a team of medical personnel around him. He turned blue, passed out, and they began CPR. After seven minutes of pure adrenaline-filled terror, he stabilized.

My wife collapsed in the hall from exhaustion. The news was grim as the doctor told Sheree, "He was out for seven minutes. We will have to see if he has brain activity in the morning"

My wife called after she has gained some composure and told me, "Come up to the hospital, your son is dying."

The two-hour drive to the hospital is the longest two hours of my life filled with unanswerable questions and uncertainty. As I walked into the room and saw Izaac for the first time, I was overcome with emotion. The sight of a child, any child, lying on a bed, swollen from fighting for their life, with an intubation tube, is enough to bring anyone to tears, especially if it is your child. He looked so helpless, uncomfortable, and lifeless. It was too much to take and I collapsed over the bed in tears.

The next day could not have come quick enough. The doctor ordered an EEG and with excitement he told us Izaac had brain activity. This was extremely exciting news, but it left us with the question of "what now?" Over time the answer to this question became "whatever it takes!"

Izaac stayed in the hospital for six weeks. Sheree would stay by his side during the week, and I would come up on Friday nights for the weekend. We would see each other on Sunday afternoon. Monday morning, I would leave the hospital at 5:30 am and drive two hours back to my house. I would take a shower, change, and head off to work. I lived in constant fear of getting a phone call from Sheree.

During the hospital stay, Izaac's neurosurgeon found a spinal stenosis (compression of the spinal cord) happening at the base of the skull.

With our consent he did a surgery to open up this space to allow the spinal cord to work properly. The surgery went off without a problem and we thought the aspiration and breathing issues he had been dealing with for the first six months were behind him. Unfortunately, we were wrong. Izaac was released from the hospital just in time for Christmas. We were extremely excited to have the family together for the holidays. Izaac was seven months old at the time.

A New Kind of Normal

In February of 2009, just a few months after Izaac's surgery, he had another major aspiration. Two days later, his breathing worsened and his oxygen levels began to drop. That night, Sheree and I decided we will sleep in shifts. I told her that I will take the first shift. I can only imagine the pain and fear that Izaac had to be feeling. He would whimper and whine on occasion when he first fell asleep, but as the hours slowly went by his whimper turned into full blown screams. Finally, the decision came to take him to the local hospital. They told us, "He is very sick and needs to be air lifted to St. Louis."

We could not ride with them so we had to drive. Once again, the unknown of what was happening in the air, somewhere above us, as we sped to the hospital was ridiculous. Sheree and I sat in silence most of the way only speaking to offer words of encouragement to each other. When we got to St. Louis, they were fast at work, saving Izaac's life, and again he was intubated at nine months.

Sleep deprived and exhausted, Sheree and I didn't know what to think or what to do, but we knew where we had to be.

Our routine started again.

I would come up on the weekend, Sheree would stay by Izaac's side during the week, and Izaac would fight for his life. Slowly, Izaac recovered over the next couple of months. Many things were tried and many problems arose. Izaac plugged off (a mucous plug in his throat) three times causing an emergency on the floor, and a figurative heart attack for us. Every time we thought he was healthy enough to take the intubation tube out, he would slowly lose oxygen and need to be re-intubated. They tried BiPAP, CPAP, breathing treatments, oxygen, removing his lymph nodes and tonsils, but nothing seemed to work. Finally, after three months of "our routine," the decision was made to give Izaac a tracheotomy with a ventilation system. This would mean that Izaac would be on life support, but we would be able to take him home. We didn't know whether we were taking him home to die or to recover which was a very scary thought.

See picture 7 on page 96

Izaac celebrated his first birthday in the cafeteria of Children's Hospital at St. Louis, MO.

See picture 8 on page 96

See picture 9 on page 97

Looking back at the first year of Izaac's life, some thoughts come to mind. I found out that the person I married—the person I vowed to spend the rest of my life with—was also the strongest person I know. It did not come without sacrifice. My wife sacrificed her career, family, and friends. My daughter lost the innocence of childhood and the idea of a family for a full year of her life. She was only two years old at the time. She celebrated her third birthday in the cafeteria of St. Louis Children's Hospital. While Izaac was in the hospital, she was passed around from house to house, grandma to aunt to grandma and back again. I hope she understands someday that we did not have a choice. I lost my family for a while and the thought of how things could have been makes me appreciate the way things are. All I knew at the time, it was the way it was. We could only take it one day at a time.

We spent Thanksgiving in the hospital and lost countless hours of sleep. We all made major sacrifices. In the end it was all for the cause—to keep Izaac alive.

After all of this chaos, we were faced with a decision. Izaac's lungs were not functioning well enough to support his body. He had been through every surgery there is to open up the airway and assist his breathing. Do we have him trached or not? Every doctor on his team said get him trached to relieve pressure off the lungs. After speaking with other parents who have had their child trached, we decided it was the only option. Just a few weeks before Izaac's first birthday, after spending almost six of his first twelve months in the hospital, he went in for surgery to get a tracheotomy. To us, this was the scariest surgery that he had dealt with up to this point. It was a surgery on his airway airway. One wrong move could have been fatal. We were left with questions. Will he be able to come home? What will we need to do to keep him safe? How will we get through this? What now? Keeping with our optimistic outlook, Sheree and I looked at each other and said, "Whatever it takes," and to this day this is how we live our lives.

The surgery was a success. Izaac was swollen, groggy, and crabby from the surgery but you could tell that he was breathing easier, which was a relief to both of us. We celebrated his first birthday in the hospital lobby and he got to eat cake. It was an emotional day for Sheree and I. Just after his first birthday with some recovery and training on the vent, we were able to take Izaac home.

Sometimes being thankful for what you have is really hard. We are conditioned in our society to want more and look for the next best thing. We have learned how to be thankful for the little things in life. If Izaac was born ten years ago, he would not have been able to come home with a portable vent. He would have had to stay in the hospital until he was healed and off the vent, which means he would still be in there. If Izaac was born twenty-five years ago, he would not have survived. So being thankful for even the time that we live in is something we are thankful for every day. I challenge individuals to take a step back and look at their life to take notice of the little things.

> What you have is more important than what you could have.
>
> —Greg Pursley

One to Two

Bringing Izaac home was bittersweet. We had grown accustomed to the schedule and routine of the hospital. We were excited to get our family back, but terrified of all of the new changes. We were now going to be fully responsible for Izaac's care. Luckily, we were given the option of having nursing help by our insurance carrier. The nursing service would allow us to make the transition from the hospital to our home. We did have to allow strangers from a nursing company to come in to our house multiple times per day which was challenging in itself, but it was definitely worth it. Izaac's schedule was and continues to be a challenging one. He had to have six breathing treatments per day, Pepcid to help with reflux, and allergy meds to reduce mucous production; we also had to give Izaac a bath, change his trach ties (holds the trach in his neck), and change his gauze (cotton that goes around the trach to prevent infection). Oh yeah, and keep him alive. It was and is a daunting, repetitive schedule that is very hard to keep up with.

Although having the trach put some of our nervous energy at ease, it also raised other feelings of uneasiness. A normal child can cry and the parent will worry about what the child wants. Is the child hungry, thirsty, dirty, or tired? We worried about all of these things also, but secondary to Izaac losing oxygen. The hardest part was the reality of the fragile state our son was in. How close he was to walking the line between life and death every also, but secondary. We found out very quickly if Izaac became disconnected from the vent, or if he was crying hard, we had about fifteen seconds to fix the situation before Izaac would turn blue. We were always on edge and it has carried over to our current lives.

The vent has multiple connections from it to Izaac. There is a connection at the vent, at the heater, and three at the trach. If any of these were to disconnect and the circuit was incomplete, he would not be able to get enough air in to his lungs due to the damage from pneumonias in the past. If the vent becomes disconnected, it sounds like a jet engine that is starting up. Looking back, it was almost comical because we knew the severity of the situation; if a disconnection occurred, Sheree, Evee-Kay, and I would sprint to the vent to reconnect it.

The first year of having him at home on the vent was a learning process. This was a new situation, a new phase of our lives we had to become comfortable with. We had to call the ambulance two times in the first year, but did not have to send him in the ambulance because we were able to resolve it at home. Considering the fragility of his state, I consider that a win. I can only attribute the lack of ambulance calls to Sheree and her ability to be reactive to Izaac's small changes. The one negative about having the trach is there is an increase in the possibility of infection—staph, strep, pseudomonas, etc. You name it and it could "grow" in his stoma site (where the trach goes in to the body). We didn't know it at the time but the winter is the worst. It is cold and dry in the outside world and his trach site is warm and moist, which is the perfect combo for germ growth. There really were more instances than I can put in the book. The simplest little change, or cough, or sneeze, or malfunction of equipment, or human error would cause an emergency.

He came home right after his birthday which is in May. Month after month, he got better and better. He was able to sustain life off of the vent for fifteen seconds, and then twenty-five seconds, and then thirty-five seconds, that is until the winter. Once again, we had to head off to the hospital in November. The good news is he already had his airway secure. The bad news is that he is so unique that the ER doctors in our local town did not really know what to do. They don't really train for a dwarf with a trach on a vent and oxygen. Luckily, we were able to work together with them and they allowed us to provide feedback for his situation. Most children have accomplishments in their first year. They learn to roll over, sit up, crawl, and sometimes even walk. In our situation it seemed every accomplishment was larger than life. We were told so many times not to expect much, so every little improvement seemed extraordinary. In his first year Izaac improved and that was enough for us. We let him grow at his own pace, expecting nothing.

The first year, we just did not know whether he was going to improve or not. We had accomplishments and setbacks. It was definitely a relief when he was able to reach his second birthday.

Two to Three

The second year promised to be better than the first. Izaac was now standing with the aid of a table or couch to hold on to. He started to roll over and develop core strength. We called it his "super roll" and posted it on YouTube. He started to put his feet and forehead on the ground with his butt in the air and lift his hands out to the sides. We would say, "Look Mom, no hands" and clap. Every new thing that he did or came up with was a new miracle. It was something that, at one point, we didn't know if he would ever be able to accomplish. His cognitive function improved and he seemed to be progressing at a steady pace. The great thing is that even though his first two years of life were full of surgeries, medical treatment, office visits, PT, OT, nurses and drug-induced comas, he was still very happy. What a miracle. Everyone knows a person who complains about everything in life. How can someone like Izaac, who has gone through all of this, end up being so thankful for life. The only way I can explain it is a miracle.

Izaac's second year was full of milestones and improvement. We were able to take him off of the vent and add a Passy-Muir Valve. This is a cap that goes on the end of the trach allowing him to breathe in through the trach and breathe out through his mouth. This is the first step on the road to getting rid of the vent and trach permanently. As parents, we were very hopeful…and looking back, probably too hopeful. We thought, *If he makes it through the winter without needing the vent, he can get the trach out next year.* Selfish is the only word I can think of about it now. We wanted him to get rid of the vent so badly that we did not see the warning signs of what was coming. Every parent wants to see their child improve and grow. In our case we wanted him to be as healthy as possible, which in our mind, meant getting off the vent as soon as possible.

When he is on the Passy-Muir Valve, he has to force the air past his trach tube and out of his nose and mouth. The side effect we now know we should have looked for is CO_2 (carbon dioxide) build up. This will change the pH of the body and put extra stress on it. In 2010, for six months, Izaac was completely off of his vent. You can imagine our anticipation of events to come. "He will be able to get off of the vent and be a 'normal' boy." We were wrong. Occasionally Izaac started to require oxygen while he slept. After a short while he started to require oxygen when he was awake. Then finally it happened. In February of 2011, Izaac had a massive infection in his lungs which required emergency response and a two-week hospital stay. Unbeknownst to us at the time this happened partly due to the CO_2 build up in his body. It seemed as if we were back to square one. Our hopes were shattered. The reality that he was not going to get the trach out any time soon set in. Looking at her own foreseeable future, Sheree slumped into a deep depression. The repetition of her days, and the thought of no ending in sight sparked the flame of depression that consumed her entire body. The infection caused long term damage to Izaacs' lungs and set his recovery back tremendously. It also set back our hopes and put a damper on our spirits.

His second year may have ended differently than we had hoped but it did not come without improvement. At almost two and one half years old Izaac took his first steps. This began the next chapter in his life, and the next set of unknowns for ours.

See picture 10 on page 97

Three to Four

A new plan was developed. We were ecstatic that there was even a possibility of a third birthday but change was in the air. Sheree and I had to make another decision. Go slow with his recovery and don't push too fast. Be selfless and think about Izaac only. Put ourselves not in the backseat or the back burner but out of the picture until Izaac is 110 percent healthy. We came to the realization that we would use the vent periodically during the day and continuously at night until he was more than stable. This would mean more responsibility for the family, but it needed to be done. We graciously accepted the challenge and have lived up to it.

Today, Izaac is happy and getting healthier every day. We are blessed to be able to have him in our lives despite all of the things we have been through. He is able to go to school with the help of a nurse. This allows him to have social interaction and develop independence. We are still very cautious about his health and we have learned a lot about how he reacts to his environment. If it gets too cold, we keep him home. If there are a lot of kids that have been sick, we will keep him home. I feel sorry for him sometimes because he has to stay home so much, but he understands it is for his health. I have to think he gets stir crazy, but then again he really doesn't know any difference. There is an old saying "What doesn't kill you makes you stronger." Izaac must be one strong kid. As I watch Evee-Kay and Izaac grow, I realize that I have learned a few things up to this point. I will never stop learning about life and this has taught me how to recognize the moments that are right in front of me. I am observing and participating in what is happening happening instead of taking each moment for granted. I am excited and nervous about what will happen in the future, but very optimistic at the same time.

As I look forward to Izaac's life, I see his realization of the differences of his life. I see him struggling with daily activities. I see him dealing with other children making fun of him, who don't understand why he is different. Some of these things make me nervous, angry, or even hurt. One thing I won't allow myself to be is scared. I choose, and I hope that I can teach my family to choose, how to accept the challenge of life and leave it a better place.

> The future is not some place we are going to, but one we are creating. The paths are not to be found, but made, and the activity of making them, changes both the maker and the destination.
>
> —John Schaar

Normal People Problems

One day, my wife and I were going to take a walk with Izaac and Evee-Kay. It was a sunny day with only a few clouds in the sky, perfect for a walk. We grabbed Izaac, his stroller, and all of the necessary medical equipments. We started packing everything up and a half an hour later, we were off. We were all in great spirit. We were playful and laughing. There was a feeling of calmness in the air. Sheree, Evee-Kay, and I walking with huge smiles on our faces feeling the warmth of the sun. Izaac, sitting in his stroller with his vent hanging off the back, suction unit and ambu-bag underneath, and oxygen on top was pointing at different things and calling them out.

"Bird," as he points to the sky.

"Tree," as he points toward the horizon.

"Lets go fishing," as he points to the lake.

Really it was a moment that we all think of when we look into the future with their family. Everyone happy, healthy, and feeling great. Sheree looked off into the horizon and said, "It looks like it might rain. How long should we walk?"

This is what I mean by normal people problems. On a family walk, most people worry about things like hydration, snacks, length of the walk, etc. Suddenly, Izaac's vent beeped which could mean a lot of different things. Like I said before, coughing, talking, breathing too fast, laughing, etc. We checked the vent and it indicated power loss. *Snap!* Back to reality. We have about fifteen minutes to get a new battery. The decision is made that they will stay where they are, and before the vent dies. I will run back to get a new battery. So the sprinting begins. As I run away, Sheree yelled, "This is not normal people problems." About ten minutes later, I came back with another battery and we hooked it up to the vent. Disaster averted. Meanwhile, Izaac has been asking, "Where is Daddy going?" totally oblivious to the situation.

It is funny how life is experienced. Tony Robbins says, "You don't experience life, you experience your associations by what you're stimulated by." We all have different life experiences which is why we all view things in a different way. Izaac's reality is what it is. He knows nothing different in life therefore it is nothing new to him. You see, it is all in the choice of our reaction. We could choose to not take a walk. We could choose to be bitter, or give up, or quit doing fun things, but we know our children are only going to be as good as what they were stimulated by in life. If they don't experience all life has to offer, when they are older they will have nothing to pull from. Nothing in their past where they can say I've experienced that and I know what to do. No failures to learn from. This is why we choose to have fun no matter what. "Normal people problems" is really just a choice that Sheree and I have made. We choose to laugh about the complicated life we have been given. We choose to face our challenges with an open mind and ask ourselves what is fun about this. Isn't that what life is about anyway—learning and having fun in the process? We have chosen to say "normal people problems" when something happens that is normal or average, and we have chosen to say "that's not normal people problems" when something happens that is not normal or average.

Most people react to things that happen to them instead of facing the situation head on and asking themselves the hard questions. There is no such thing as a perfect day. If you wake up today and say to yourself, "Today is going to be perfect," you have set yourself up for failure, and your only choice is to react to problems that come your way. If you wake up today and say to yourself, "Today is not going to be perfect, and that's okay," your life will change. As long as you have the viewpoint of "No matter what happens, I am going to learn from it," your days will be much better. This is what I have chosen to do every day. My motto is whatever happens, use it! "normal people problems" or not.

What Is Dwarfism?

Dwarfism is a reduction of height of an individual due to a bone growth abnormality. It is not an intellectual impairment. Dwarfism is the medical term applied to someone with this bone growth disorder. There are over two hundred types of dwarfism. Midget is a derogatory term and is considered this way due to the history of how the term was used. The commonly accepted and politically correct term for anyone less than four feet and eleven inches tall is a little person. A little person has typically the same IQ level as that of an average size person, but there are certain health complications that are associated with a child born with dwarfism. Lack of muscle tone, medically referred to as hypotonia, is a common condition that is observed in most people affected with dwarfism. Other medical complications include delayed motor skills, breathing problems, painful joints and spine, arthritis, frequent ear infections, crowding of teeth, weight problems, and hydrocephalus (water on the brain). Some types of dwarfism are an inherited genetic condition, and in some types it's a deficient hormone causing the short stature. Over two hundred types of dwarfism range from less serious to fatal. The most common type is achondroplasia which, when broken down, means no bone growth. This means that the bones are not capable of producing bone correctly.

Over 80 percent of people diagnosed with dwarfism have average height parents with no history of dwarfism in the family. It is thought to occur by a random genetic mutation in the third trimester of pregnancy but at the moment no one knows for sure.

Acceptable terms for dwarfism are dwarf, little person, or short statured. People with dwarfism can lead normal lives with average life expectancies, although most have many medical issues.

There are two main categories of dwarfism which are disproportionate dwarfism and proportionate dwarfism.

Disproportionate dwarfism causes abnormal development of the body parts, usually short arms and legs with a normal size torso. In proportionate dwarfism, nearly all the body parts are small to the same extent, giving a proportioned body stature.

Major forms of dwarfism include: Achondroplasia, diastrophic dysplasia, spondyloepiphyseal dysplasia, primordial dwarfism, pseudoachondroplasia, hypochondroplasia, pituitary dwarfism, osteogenesis imperfecta, Turner syndrome, and psychogenic dwarfism.

Statistically, different types of dwarfism occur with different frequency. Achondroplasia, the form Izaac has, occurs at a rate of about one in fifty thousand. If you were at a major sporting event and the stadium was full of people, there would be one person out of all of the people in the stadium with dwarfism.

I could go on for days about all of the different types of dwarfism and how they are different from each other, but that is another subject all together. If you have other questions or would like to learn more, you can contact the LPA (Little People of America) at www.lpaonline.org

Our Successful Relationship

Did you know that over 80 percent of all marriages with a special needs child ends in divorce? (Dr. Laura Marshak and Fran Prezant, authors of *Married with Special-Needs Children*). I never understood the dynamics of this until I was thrown into the mix. I have to ask myself at this point, how did we make it where others have failed? Some might suggest that our situation is not as hard as others. Some would say that it was luck or that we are just really stubborn. The secret is as old as time. We stick by three principles—faith, trust, and communication.

In a "normal" marriage, faith, trust, and communication are very important, but in a marriage where there is constant interruption, where the focus is continuously turned toward keeping your child alive, faith, trust, and communication become the key that will be needed to keep unlocking the door of the relationship. Believe me, that door keeps trying to shut right in your face. Sheree and I started out as young, carefree, but still responsible individuals. I was twenty-one, and she was twenty-three. We always lived in fast forward.

We met in February and within the first two months, we took a random, unplanned trip to Springfield, MO. Upon arriving at our destination, we realized that we had friends in Dallas, TX so we decided to take a detour on our road trip. When we arrived at the visitor's bureau to see what Dallas had to offer, we were told the St. Louis Cardinals were playing against the Houston Astros that evening.

"How long does it take to get to Houston from here?" I asked.

"About three hours," the travel guide responded.

"And game time is how long from now?"

"Three hours."

Without any hesitation, Sheree and I whipped our heads around, made eye contact and without even making a sound we raced to the car like kids who were told they would get candy if they were in their seatbelts in five seconds. We giggled like children most of the road trip. Rain, heat, clouds, or fog couldn't damper our spirits. It was truly meant to be. After hitting Houston, we decided we were only a half an hour from the beach so we then went to Galveston. It was windy and a little chilly, but it didn't matter. We made fun out of any situation. At this point, we had only known each other for a couple of months, but it didn't seem to matter.

That weekend, I truly fell in love. There is a song that says, "When you love a woman, you understand her, you can feel it in her touch," which is true. To this day, even though our situation has changed, she still gives me goose bumps with every glance, touch, and smile.

While in Galveston, we noticed a wedding chapel and one of us made the comment. "Wouldn't it be funny if we got back to St. Louis and we were married?" Normally, that statement would have sent both of us running for the hills faster than superman himself. But a calm feeling came over both of us as we contemplated the thought. I turned thinking she would be trembling from fear, but both of us just looked at each other, smiled, locked hands, and went on our way walking down the side walk with a new found hope on life like we could accomplish anything.

Our relationship started, and continues with great faith, trust, and communication. Think about trust. A lack of trust will lead to doubt, questions, concern, and a general feel of deception. A lack of trust can kill any conversation, friendship, or relationship. How can you talk with someone whom you have a lack of trust with?

Constantly, you will be asking yourself questions about what they are saying. You will be judging the credibility of every word, statement, story, and thought of the other participant in the conversation. A lack of trust will lead to wasted time also. Constantly checking up, worried about where the other person is going, their e-mail, text messages, and so on. Honesty is truly the best policy when it comes to a successful relationship. Trust is something that most people give freely until it is broken. It can be mended once it is broken, but there will always be a visible scar. This is one of the ways Sheree and I have been able to keep our relationship going and defy the odds. The unwavering and fearless way we pass along any information to each other without fear of being judged or persecuted in any way is the only way to be in a relationship.

Trust can only be accomplished through proper communication. Communication is more than just a passing of words from one to the other. Communication is a process where one individual passes information to the other. The one receiving the information computes it, comprehends it, and then responds to it. There are other forms of communication other than just the spoken word. Body language plays an important role in communication also. Have you ever seen someone visibly upset but they haven't said a word? This is body language. My philosophy is if someone is showing you they are upset then obviously they want you to react to it. This is why when my wife looks upset, I persist on helping her come to a solution to her problem. This can only be accomplished through great communication. The most important of these is faith. I am not just talking about faith in each other. I am also talking about faith in God himself. Faith there is a future in front of you and even though times are hard, better times await you. When you have complete faith you will find an internal peace unmatched by anything else in this earth.

A breakdown of these three principles is the reason why over 80 percent of couples with special needs children split up. There is so much chaos on a regular basis that if these three principles are not the strong foundation of the relationship is sure to crumble.

Life is messy and marriage is no different. With divorce rates higher than ever, you have to ask yourself, why? If you walk into a marriage expecting it to be perfect, then you are setting yourself up for failure. You cannot expect perfection in life because nothing in life is perfect. I think a lot of people get married thinking it is going to be this wonderful, beautiful, perfect union. That is not life, and it will not work. When I speak at events, I talk about a perfect day. Ask yourself this question. "Is anything in life perfect?" I asked myself this question and found out that everything in life is imperfect. If you wake up and think that the day will be perfect, well, then you are setting yourself up for failure in your day. I wake up and say, "No matter what happens, today is going to be great." The other issue in marriage is selfishness. If you can get the point that being in a marriage is putting the other person's needs before yourself, then you will have a greater chance of success.

I am not an expert in marriages or relationships, I am just talking about common sense things that in my opinion have been lost over generations. To me, the secret of a great relationship or marriage comes down to four principles that my wife and I live by—faith, communication, selflessness, and trust. Look at your own relationship. How well do these fit in? Be honest and if they don't I fit would ask myself, "How can I fit these with yourself in to my relationship?" I can tell you from my personal experience, if we did not have these principles in our daily lives, we would not be married today.

What We Have Learned

The old saying goes "When life hands you lemons, make lemonade," but what if it is bigger and more complex? Coming out of this, the best question I can ask is "What did we learn from this experience?" I have found a new outlook in life. No more "Why did this happen to me" or "Knowing my luck." Life is what you make it.

Change your thoughts, change your life. I have heard this statement from many motivational speakers and life coaches. The funny thing is that it is so true. Change how you think about any situation and your whole life will change. The great thing about this is you have the power… you have the power to make any change in your life. So many people sit back and allow the world to control them. I have heard people say things like, "I don't have any money." Well, who's fault is that? Is it your employers? Is it your parents? Is it your significant others? No. If you don't think you have enough money, the only person you have to blame is you. I hear people say, "I can't do that."

Confucius says, "Those who say they can, and those who say they can't are both generally right."

By making such a bold statement like "I can't," your brain says you're right. This does not only inhibit you from achieving whatever you are saying you can't do, but it also lowers your self-esteem, self-worth, and any amount of motivation you may have. I heard of a cycle one time that has opened my eyes. It says that if you don't believe that something will work, how much effort will you put in to it? Will you put all of your effort? 110 percent? If you don't believe something will work, you are not going to put all of your effort in to it. There will be a voice that comes up in your head that says "I can't do that;" "That won't work;" "What's the point? This is not going to get us anywhere." Most of us face this issue constantly. After you say it won't work or I can't and you don't put the amount of effort in to it as if you were totally committed, what kind of results will you get? Terrible results, most likely. How does it make you feel when you get terrible results? Terrible, like a failure, worthless, etc. So then your brain says, "See, I said it wouldn't work and it didn't work, so I was right." This just confirms what you had originally said, which is negative. If you practice negativity, you will get negativity.

The opposite also holds true. If you believe with all of your heart something is going to work, you will put more effort in to it than you knew you had. With the extra effort you will get more results, which will then confirm in your mind what you had said in the beginning. "See, I said this would work and this worked so let's work on something even bigger and better." This is a positive spiral moving you toward motivation and achievement. If you practice positivity, you will get positivity.

The point is we are what we think we are. We do what we think we can accomplish. It all starts with our thoughts. The moment you think something about yourself, it is true. *I think I am fat, I think I am worthless, I think I don't belong.* The thoughts turn into what you believe which turn into your reality in life. I have walked into a room where I was totally out of place and decided that I fit in and I was going to have fun anyway. With this thought, I fit in and that's the way it was. If I thought I didn't fit in, I would have acted awkward and people would have noticed it, which would have just fueled the awkwardness. The point is your thoughts dictate your beliefs which create your reality and who you are.

We live in an age today where information is so available. We live in the easiest country to succeed in the world. If you don't have money, food, clothing, a house, etc., there are programs available to you in any city across the country to help out. There are free libraries that you can go to and do research on the internet to learn about anything. I did this when I started typing this book. I am not a trained author. I did not know how the process of getting a book published worked, but I had a passion to tell this story to the world in hopes it would help people overcome their own demons and obstacles in life. I simply got on the internet and started looking up how the process works. I made the decision to do it though. You can do the same with anything.

So what is it that you want? Do you want to lose weight? Do you want to change something in your life? Do you want to change your finances? What is it going to be from now on? Every day, you have a choice to make. We can make the choice today and every day to be great or mediocre. Our lives are not made up of great moments alone. They are made up of the accumulation of moments no matter how small. I have realized each moment matters, and each moment you let slip away is a moment you could have made yourself or someone else better. So I challenge you to be the person you can be, and not the person you have settled to be.

> I compete with the best I can be. That is why I am better than everyone.
>
> —Michael Jordan

Life's Purpose

I met a girl who changed my life at Children's Hospital in St. Louis, MO. During Izaac's three-month stay there in 2009, I would take my guitar and play music to him. It was almost like a release for him to forget about what was going on. The room was nice, with a window and curtains, a makeshift bed, a TV, and a private bathroom, but it was still the hospital. I would get there on a Friday afternoon and Sheree would immediately leave to get some sleep at her mom's. I remember thinking about what we would be able to do while we were there.

"Izaac, do you want to watch SportsCenter?"

He would shake his head no.

"Izaac, do you want to sit up?"

He would shake his head no again.

"Izaac, do you want to play guitar?"

He would shake his head yes.

He didn't like to feel enclosed in his room so we would have the door open. He really liked to see what was happening outside in the hallway. He was and is very observant. About every thirty minutes, a nurse would have to come in and take vitals or check on him in some way and I would just keep on playing. One day, a nurse looked up at me and said, "I don't want to bother you but can I ask a favor?"

"Absolutely," I replied with excitement. I love to help people out and to tell the truth, I don't do well sitting around.

"There is this girl on the other side of this floor that has cystic fibrosis. She is nineteen and her lungs are starting to fail her. The only thing she wants in this life is to get married and a boy from her school said he would."

This was not a real marriage with a marriage certificate but more of a formality to fulfill her dreams.

"Can I meet her?" I said with excitement. I love helping people, and I love projects.

The nurse replied, "I will have to clear it with her doctor because of infection risk."

The doctor gave me the go ahead as long as I wore scrubs, a face mask, shoe covers, gloves, and had not been sick recently. I remember walking down the hall thinking to myself, *Am I ready for this with all that I am going through?* I was excited, scared, and anxious all at the same time. I felt as nervous as if I was going to be speaking in front of thousands of people and yet I couldn't wait. As I walked in, I saw a frail girl with an oxygen cannula on, sitting at the end of the bed clipping out pictures from wedding magazines.

"Hello, Ashley. The nurses mentioned to me that you have a wedding coming up. Is this true?"

She nodded slowly, barely having the strength to hold up her head.

"I play guitar and sing. I wrote a song called "Angel By My Side." Would you like to hear it?"

All she could muster was a small grin, but I could tell she wanted to jump with excitement. We only had a few minutes to talk but I told her I would get her a CD. "Angel By My Side" is a song that I wrote for my wife on our wedding day and now it was taking on a new meaning. It was no longer just about my wife, the song was about something bigger than just us. Sheree said, "The song was perfect for Ashley."

The day of the wedding was a beautiful one. It was held in the garden on the fifth floor of Children's Hospital. Everyone was ready and in there places. The doctors had agreed that she could proceed. Imagine, if you can, a thin, frail, but beautiful girl with the odds against her. Somehow, she is finding the will to push through a loss of oxygen and tremendous physical pain to walk the fifty steps to get to the altar. As I played my song, I watched her struggle to get down the aisle and could barely get through the song without bursting into tears. There was not a dry eye in the place, and it was one of the most beautiful and heart wrenching events in my life. There were doctors, nurses, family, and strangers coming together for the joy of a woman who had overcome so much.

A couple of years later, I heard that Ashley received a double lung transfusion, and I pray not only for her, but for anyone in a similar situation.

The point is that all too often we limit ourselves based on what we think we can accomplish. The truth is we are only limited by our beliefs about ourselves. Our ideas about ourselves, our truths in life, and our ideas about what is good and bad are all based on our individual life experiences and therefore our beliefs. Ashley believed she could do something. She prepared herself for it, and even though the doctors thought it was a bad idea, she did it anyway. Her will and her reason why was so strong it would overcome whatever was thrown at it. What if your reason why was that strong? I hear it all of the time about weight loss, finances, exercises, home repairs, etc. I don't have "time" or "money" or "energy" or "resources." What they are really saying is "I don't have a strong enough reason; therefore, it is not important enough for me to change who I am." Who we are is only what we believe we are. I learned from a great man named Robert Kiyosaki the saying "Be, Do, Have." Who do you have to be, to do the things you need to do, He learned it from Napolean Hill in the book "Think and grow rich" to have the things you want to have?

You are who you are today because of the decisions you have made in your life. There are things that happen in life beyond your control, but you have the power to choose how you will deal with those things. Sheree and I chose to view our son as a positive. We chose to look at him with unconditional love and make the best of every day.

Life is hard and there are no perfect days. There can be great days, but not perfect days. If you expect every day to be perfect, you set yourself up for disappointment. Expect to fail. Expect to have hard times. When something comes at you that you weren't expecting, learn from it. Laugh at it. Robert Kiyosaki also says, "Someday I will laugh at this." Why wait until someday? Laugh now." You only have one today; one this second, minute, hour, day, week, month, etc. Make the most of it. Life is just a journey…a time for learning, failing, correcting, and growing. People get so caught up in what they are not happy about in their lives that they forget to look around and be where they are at that moment. I know because I was there and observe it in people all of the time.

If there is anything to learn from this book, I hope you will see your situation is not unique. There is someone else out there going through the same issues you have. Find those people and talk about what you are going through. Don't try and solve your life's problems by yourself because you will have a hard time doing it. Life is a team sport and when you see someone else is on the same team as you, you will learn from your mistakes quicker, and learn more from them.

Dr. Greg Pursley

Take a page out of Ashley's book. Find your purpose and live it to the fullest. I am blessed that I have been able to find my purpose in life. I had to first make the choice to accept whatever comes at me in life and use it, and I make that choice every day. You can too. Just make the decision.

> Physical matter has limitations, but your Spirit is unlimited.
>
> —Greg Pursley

A New Kind of Normal

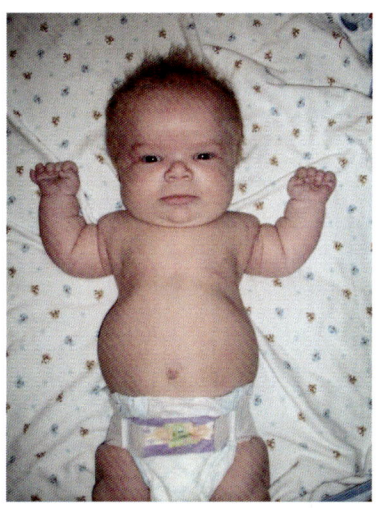

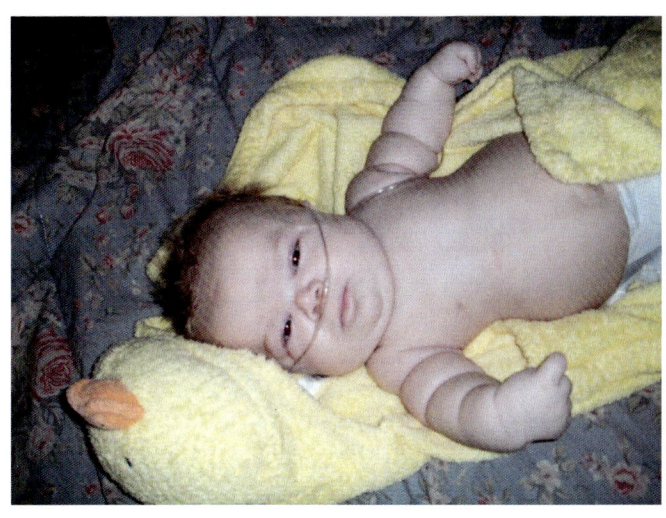

Dr. Greg Pursley

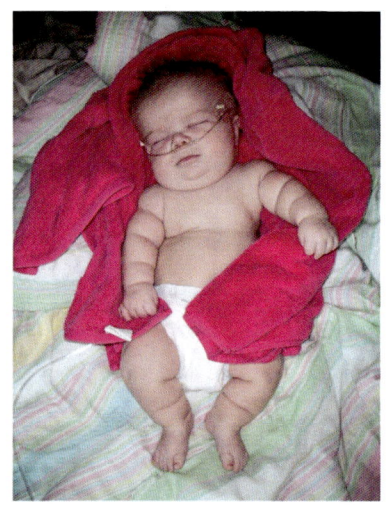

A New Kind of Normal

Dr. Greg Pursley

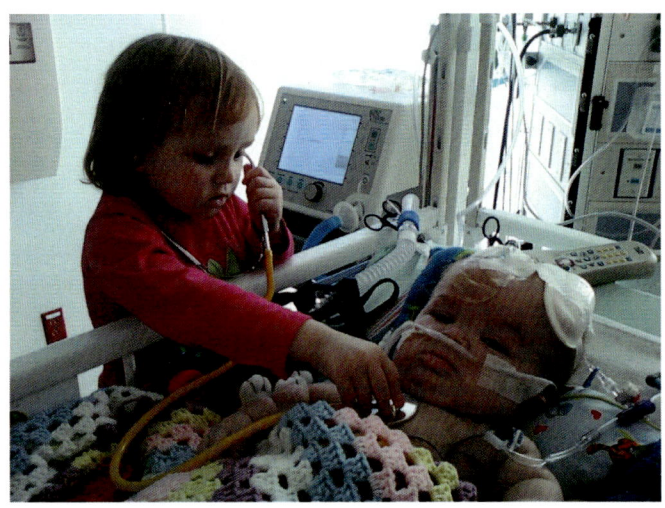

A New Kind of Normal

Dr. Greg Pursley

A New Kind of Normal

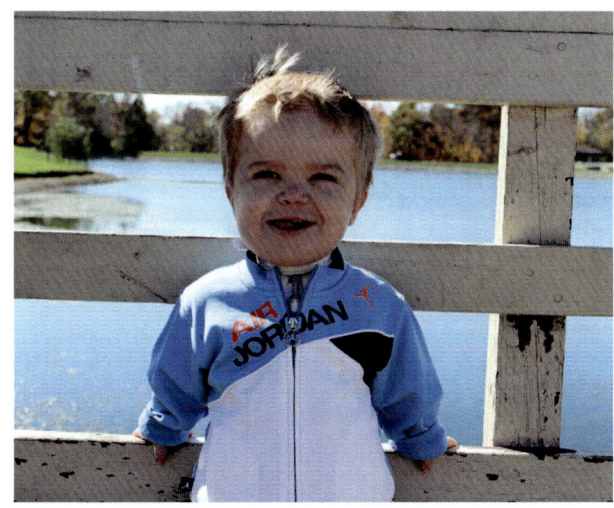

Dr. Greg Pursley

A New Kind of Normal

Dr. Greg Pursley

A New Kind of Normal

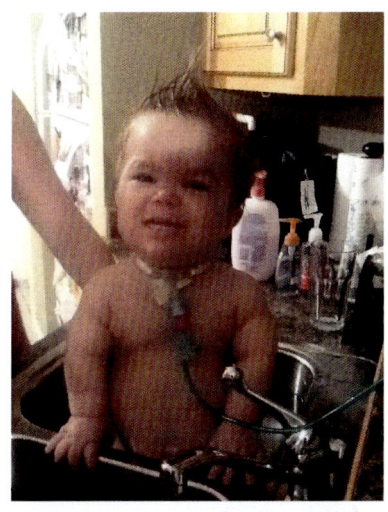

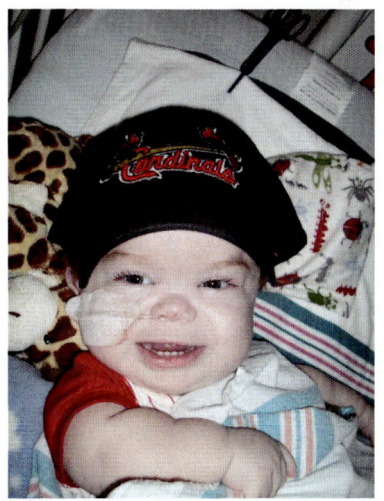

Dr. Greg Pursley

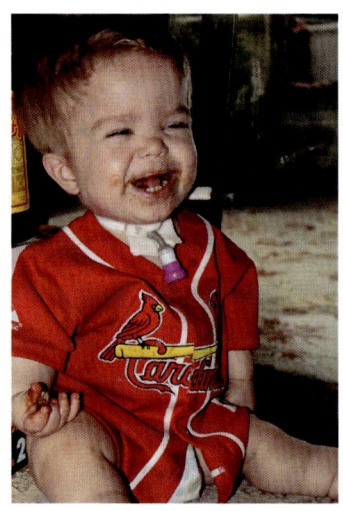

A New Kind of Normal

Dr. Greg Pursley